Blyth Voices

Folk songs
collected in Southwold
by Ralph Vaughan Williams in 1910

Published by the
East Anglian Traditional Music Trust

Published by the East Anglian Traditional Music Trust

EATMT, 44 Old Street, Haughley, Stowmarket, Suffolk IP14 3NX

First published 2003

ISBN 0 9545943 0 4

Edited by Katie Howson
Music set by Jeannie Harris and Alex Bartholomew
Biographical research by Katie Howson
Design by John Howson
Printed by Gipping Press, Needham Market, Suffolk

A folksong is like a tree, whose stem dates back from immemorial times, but which continually puts out new shoots.'

Ralph Vaughan Williams, English Folk Songs, 1912

Acknowledgements

For generous help with the research, and photographs of Ralph Vaughan Williams and George Butterworth: the Vaughan Williams Memorial Library at the English Folk Dance and Song Society.

For permission to publish songs from her late husband's collection: Ursula Vaughan Williams.

For inspiration, information and interpretation of the songs: Chris Coe

For information and research: Roy Palmer, Martin Graebe and Mike Yates

For support, research and photographs: Southwold Town Council, Southwold Museum and St Edmundsbury Borough Council

For photographs from their family collections: Andrew Jenkins and Gary May

For information regarding singing in Southwold: John Winter, Trevor Ray and Jim Blythe

For financial support for the Blyth Valley Voices project:
Awards for All,
Britten-Pears Foundation, Suffolk County Council, Waveney District Council, Suffolk Coastal District Council

Contents

Introduction

This book contains fourteen songs which were noted down in 1910 by the composers and folk song collectors Ralph Vaughan Williams and George Butterworth in the area around Southwold on the Suffolk coast. A number have not been previously published, and in each case there has been a fair amount of research needed to match words and tunes. Publishing them together, as here, gives a sense of place and time in away that few other historical artefacts can do.

Here are songs of courtship and tragedy, with a strong flavour of the sea, as is to be expected from an area where fishing and coastal trading was as important as the holiday business in the nineteenth century. The reader may be surprised to find the stories told in these songs to be tough and even gruesome in some cases; there are shipwrecks, robbery, adultery, the threat of violence and even murders. A popular perception of folk song is that it can be rather twee and precious: this collection evidences the working populace's interest in the seamier side of life, which may be said to have its modern day equivalent in the tabloid press.

The songs are grouped so that the reader can see the range of songs performed by each singer, but it is likely that the songs noted down make up only a proportion of their repertoires. It is also inportant to remember that these were working people who sang to entertain their own families and communities in an era before radio, film and television became influences on musical taste and style.

Some of the songs are known to be very ancient, but it is often difficult to be precise about their age, because although they are sometimes found in print (most frequently on single ballad-sheets or broadsides) they also existed in an oral tradition where people learned songs from listening to each other, and the broadside printers sometimes published songs that were already in oral circulation.

Writing in 1912, in a pamphlet entitled *English Folk Songs*, Vaughan Williams commented on this oral tradition:

'One man sings to several more, they sing again their versions to others; these versions ... would probably vary considerably as the artistic instinct of the singer suggested ...'

and

'The more I see of folk-song, the more important I believe the impress of the individual to be.'

This is contrary to many a lay-person's view of folk-song as something archaic to be preserved exactly as found, but is in fact the essence of the genre, and this 'impress of the individual' is indeed to be found in abundance in the songs collected in Southwold.

This book was conceived as part of a larger project, Blyth Valley Voices, which also included an exhibition containing further information on Southwold at the time of Vaughan Williams' visit and on traditional singing and music-making in the area during the rest of the twentieth century. The other crucial part of the project was to get these songs off the page and sung again in the area from which they were collected. Chris Coe was instrumental both in this process and in the preparatory stages of working out how the sometimes fragmentary texts fitted to the wonderful tunes! As a result of the project, a number of groups and individuals now sing these songs, and we hope will continue to do so for many years.

The East Anglian Traditional Music Trust is dedicated to the development of the folk music, song and dance of the eastern counties of England and may be contacted at 44 Old Street, Haughley, Stowmarket, Suffolk IP14 3NX.

Notes on interpretation and performance

The scores are very much as noted down by Ralph Vaughan Williams and George Butterworth, with only occasional changes made to fit more closely to the lyrics in a very few cases. Key signatures are also as noted down in 1910, but these may not be the original singing keys. It is certainly acknowledged that Butterworth, at least, would note down songs in a key which meant that they would fit conveniently on the stave.

Both men occasionally noted variants to the tune: these would be in different verses where the singer adjusted the metre or the melody to fit the words. A singer of these songs should always be aware that the story takes precedence, and the tune can be bent subtly to accommodate the phrasing of words.

The influence of folk song on Ralph Vaughan Williams

The music of Ralph Vaughan Williams (1872-1958), quintessential English composer, owed much to the traditional folk songs of England. Many of his pieces were inspired, not by dusty manuscripts in archives, but by hearing such songs directly from elderly country people, and Vaughan Williams visited, listened to and noted down songs from shepherds, fishermen and agricultural labourers in his mission to shape a truly English style of classical music. Some of Vaughan Williams' compositions directly inspired by folk songs include: Norfolk Rhapsodies (1906), Fantasia on English Folk Songs (1910), Lark Ascending (1920), Six Studies in Folk Song (1926), Fantasia on Greensleeves (1934), Five Variants of Dives and Lazarus (1939) and Folk Songs of the Four Seasons (1949). These works of course represent only a proportion of his oeuvre, which, as well as many other vocal and orchestral works, included the publication of books such as *The English Hymnal* and *The Oxford Book of Carols.* Throughout his life folk song remained a vital concern, indeed in the last year of his life he was working on *The Penguin Book of English Folk Songs* with A.L. Lloyd. The folksong collector Lucy Broadwood (member of the family renowned for the manufacture of keyboard instruments) was a family friend, and she and her books *Sussex Songs* (1889) and *English County Songs* (1893) were substantial influences on the young Vaughan Williams. In the early years of the twentieth century he travelled around the country lecturing on such subjects as

'The Characteristics of National Songs in the British Isles', often with Lucy singing examples. One lecture series in 1903 took him to Brentwood in Essex, and at nearby Ingrave, Vaughan Williams was introduced, at a tea party in the Rectory, to Charles Potiphar, a 74 year old retired labourer, from whom he noted down a folk song for the first time.

Vaughan Williams' contributions to folk song research

In the ensuing decade Vaughan Williams noted down folk songs, using paper and pencil, (although he did occasionally experiment with early recording equipment, which Percy Grainger used more extensively at that time) in various parts of England, including at least ten visits to the eastern counties between 1903 and 1911. He also visited Hampshire, Sussex and Surrey and areas further north, in total noting down 790 songs and 237 texts, making a significant contribution to our national store of such songs. Vaughan Williams was of the opinion that it was essential to save these tunes from being extinguished by changes in modern society, but that similar texts could usually be found in libraries, on broadsides and ballad sheets which were published in huge numbers in the nineteenth century. From an early twenty-first century perspective we might appreciate the linguistic as well as the melodic variations formed by an oral tradition and might also wish for more details about the singers, but those were not Vaughan Williams' primary concerns. His interests were clearly focussed on the melodies of folk *songs*, although he did occasionally note down instrumental pieces such as *The Liverpool Hornpipe* on his trip to Southwold. Vaughan Williams was an active member of both the Folk Song Society (founded in 1898) and the English Folk Dance Society, from its inception in 1911. The two amalgamated in 1932, a procedure fraught with difficulties, in which Vaughan Williams was said to act as a bridge between the two groups. In 1930, the headquarters of what became the English Folk Dance and Song Society were opened in London, called after the great collector of folk song and dance, Cecil Sharp, and after Vaughan Williams' death in 1958, the library at Cecil Sharp House was named the Vaughan Williams Memorial Library.

The visit to Southwold

On his visit to Southwold, Vaughan Williams was accompanied by his friend George Butterworth, a younger man whose life was tragically cut short in the First World War, and who might otherwise have ranked alongside Sharp and Vaughan Williams as a major folksong collector in his own right. Butterworth was also a composer, but unfortunately he destroyed many of his compositions before enlisting in the army.

On Monday 24th October 1910 Butterworth and Vaughan Williams went to Shadingfield to visit a 'Mrs Keble' before carrying on to Southwold itself, where they stayed overnight, having travelled up from London on the train with their bicycles.

It seems likely that they came to Southwold at the suggestion of John Gooding, resident of the town, who was in correspondence later in 1910 with Vaughan Williams over the words to a song. They may even have stayed with Gooding, as he and his brother Donald had quite a substantial house at 49 High Street, and they evidently knew the Hurr family, who were the focal point for the visit, as Donald had collected some ghost stories from the singers' father, William Hurr in 1903.

In the evening of the 24th, Vaughan Williams noted down eleven songs from three of William's sons, William Hurr, Robert Hurr and Ben Hurr.

On Tuesday 25th October they revisited William & Robert Hurr, went on to Reydon to see a Mr Newby, then moved on to Filby, near Caister in Norfolk and finished up the following day at nearby Rollesby. This was a return visit to Norfolk for George Butterworth, who had visited the same area to collect songs with Francis Jekyll in April of that year, and he and Vaughan Williams also collected a number of songs on this trip.

Singing, audiences and locations

Folk songs usually tell a story, and as such entertain an audience, whether in a pub, at a family party or on board a boat. In the days before recorded music, when people made their own entertainment to a large extent, and when life was less crammed with information, ballads of eight or ten verses were frequently memorised. Many singers would also feature at least one sentimental song and one comic song in their repertoire, although these lighter-hearted items were not always noted down by the early folk song collectors, particularly as some were of relatively recent origin at the time, coming from the music hall and minstrel era. One Norfolk fisherman boasted that in a six-week trawling trip, he could sing two songs every evening without repeating himself. Sam Hurr, younger brother of the singing Hurrs, worked for skipper James Spence, who was described in an obituary in the Southwold Magazine in 1924 as being distinguished *'not least by the inexhaustible selection of songs which cheered the passage home'*. The songs noted down by Vaughan Williams and Butterworth probably represent only a part of the singers' repertoires.

Where Vaughan Williams met up with the Hurrs is not known, certainly in other places he went into pubs, and he may have done so on this occasion. Given that they met on two consecutive days, it is possible that the first occasion was in a pub, followed up by a quieter session to check out details (in the case of William's singing of *Lovely Joan*, Vaughan Williams wrote it out a second time). The Southwold Arms was a big pub for singing many years before this and also after it, and the White Horse would also have been a good bet for a singsong when in Charles Newby's hands a dozen or so years before this date, but where the men gathered for a drink and a song in 1910 is not known; from oral sources the Red Lion on South Green seems a possibility.

The singers and their songs

All three of the Hurrs were fishermen, from a large family going back generations in the town of Southwold. Their fortunes were mixed, their father William having suffered setbacks all through his life: the most traumatic perhaps being the sinking of his fishing punt the *Susannah* in 1893, with two of his sons on board, followed only a month later by the death of his wife.

The Hurrs intermarried with other local families such as the Palmers and the

Lowseys, and it was common practice to christen children with more than one forename, frequently with their mother's maiden name as a middle name. Forenames were also passed on from generation to generation, and to avoid confusion, men in particular were often known by nicknames.

The period preceding Vaughan Williams' visit was one of change for the brothers; their father died in 1908, and by 1910 their financial situation was such that all three owned their own small fishing boats: William had the *Vigilant*, Robert the *Boy Billy* and Ben the *Happy Thought*. These were all longshore luggers, around 2 tons, which would have been used no more than a couple of miles offshore to catch herring, sprats, shrimps, sole, cod and mackerel in season, and moored on the beach (although the harbour had been rebuilt in 1907, it was mostly used by small coastal freighters and there were 120 open boats recorded as still working off the beach in that year). Happily for Vaughan Williams, bad weather prevented most small fishing boats from putting to sea during the period of his visit in 1910. According to the Halesworth Times on November 1st, *'light fishing continued at Southwold on Saturday, and taking the week through, the results were far from satisfactory. Many boats either spoilt or lost whole fleets of nets during the earlier part of the week, and consequently several luggers had to remain in harbour over the weekend awaiting new nets.'*

We too have reason to be grateful for the bad weather at that time, otherwise Vaughan Williams may have left Southwold disappointed, and these voices from the past would have been lost to us.

Two views of 9-11 Victoria Street, Southwold

This building, which since 1933 has housed Southwold Museum, was previously two cottages. In the late nineteenth century and early twentieth century, singer William Hurr and his family lived at no. 9: his front door would have been the present museum entrance. Note the nets drying in the yard where the museum library now stands. The two children must be William's daughter Susannah, and son Sam, dating the picture to about 1900.
Photograph by Frederick Jenkins, courtesy of Andrew Jenkins

William Hurr

William Watson Hurr (1843-1925) was the eldest son of William and Maria, and like his younger brothers, born and buried in Southwold. In 1901, William, known as 'Dubber', lived in what is now the Southwold Museum, which was then divided into two tiny cottages later condemned as unfit for housing. By 1912 however, he was installed in a much more spacious home at Caterer House at 39 Victoria Street where his wife Matilda was the landlady of holiday apartments, a line of business shared by at least two of her sisters-in-law. During the First World War, 'Dubber' showed the indomitable Hurr spirit by refusing to follow war-time regulations to refrain from night fishing. His son William Samuel Thomas (known as Sam) was one of the first *not* to follow in the family tradition of fishing, and after William's death, his boat the *Vigilant* passed to his nephew, Ben's son William Albert Benjamin (the need for those nicknames becomes apparent!).

William 'Dubber' Hurr, 1910
According to a description from 1841, William's father and two uncles all had brown hair, hazel eyes and a round face with a dark complexion, and all three were approximately 5'5" tall. William seems to have the family look. He is standing outside the fishermen's lookout on Kilcock Cliff, where the public conveniences are now situated. Until the nineteen twenties the beach was lined with fishermen's huts and sheds.
Photograph by Frederick Jenkins, courtesy of Andrew Jenkins

The Loss of the London

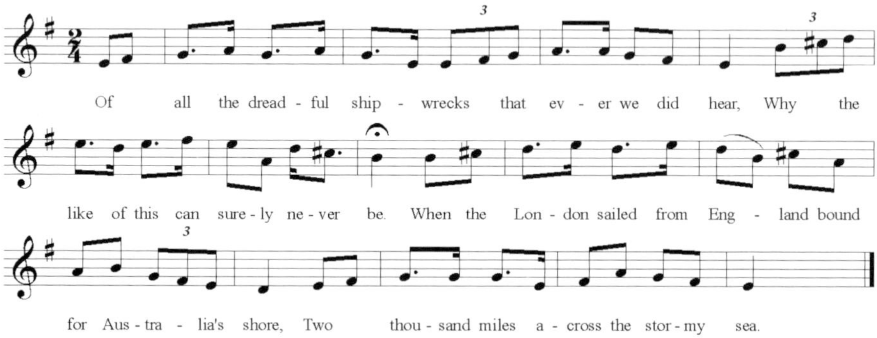

1. Of all the dreadful shipwrecks that ever we did hear,
The likes of this can surely never be.
When the London sailed from England bound for Australia's shore,
Two thousand miles across the stormy sea.

2. On the 19th December we sailed from Plymouth Bay,
Our hearts they were so happy and so gay;
We shook hands with our friends, kissed our parents so kind,
Then old England we soon did leave behind.

3. We had some pleasant weather as the coast we sailed around,
Soon for deep water we were bound.
But the stormy winds did blow and the seas ran mountains high,
On a day in the Bay of Biscay-o.

4. Then says our Captain, 'We'll haul around the ship
And run back home to Plymouth for relief.'
But the stormy winds did blow and the seas ran mountains high,
From that dreadful Bay we found we could not fly.

5. Day after day, the storm it did increase
And we all begged and prayed to be released;
Till on the third of January, that awful, fateful day,
All our masts and our sails were blown away.

6. Our good Captain Martin, he said with grief and pain,
"Our pumps they are working, but all in vain."
Then the roaring wind and waves dashed through our engine room,
Put out our fires and then we knew our doom.

7. One man there was who played a hero's part,
He pumped as if he had a lion's heart.
Brooke was the young man's name, our words will shout his fame,
He worked until all hope of life was gone,
then he calmly paced the deck all alone.

8. We lowered a lifeboat to the vessel's side,
With nineteen men to battle with the tide;
We called for our captain but we called all in vain:
"With those on board I will still remain,

9. "God speed, God speed," he cried, "Go safely to the land -
With those on board I'll die like any man."
Two hundred souls were lost in a final furious gust,
Then the London went down to rise no more.

10. Nineteen escaped in that boat that night,
For twenty long hours there was no ship in sight.
Our hearts filled with despair but then our boat was spied,
We were taken on board and with joy we cried.

11. Back at Plymouth we were quickly put ashore -
We thanked our saviours o'er and o'er.
Such a fearful loss as this, we hope you'll never hear,
For those on board we pray you'll shed a tear.

Several other sets of words were published by broadside printers in the nineteenth century under this title (or *The Wreck of the London*) but the few lines sung by William Hurr don't seem to be directly related. The words above were compiled from broadside versions, by Chris Coe during the Blyth Valley Voices project to fit Hurr's dramatic and soulful tune. The words to the first verse are those collected from William Hurr in 1910, and the few other lines noted down by Vaughan Williams are also incorporated within the text.

The *London* was an auxiliary steamship completed in 1864. On her third voyage in December 1865 she left Gravesend bound for Australia. She sank in January 1866 in a storm in the Bay of Biscay and most of the two hundred or so passengers and crew were drowned.

Lovely Joan

1. A story to you I will relate,
Concerning of a pretty maid,
Concerning of sweet lovely Joan,
As she sat milking all alone.

2. A knight mounted on a milk white steed,
So merrily, merrily he did ride,
He rode, he rode, himself all alone,
Until he came to lovely Joan.

3. "Good morning to you my pretty maid."
"Twice good morning kind sir," she said.
"Are you going milking all alone?"
"Oh yes," replied sweet lovely Joan.

4. Then he pulled out a purse of gold,
And said "Pretty maid, all this behold,
All this I'd give with me to wed."
Her cheeks they blushed like roses red.

5. "Oh no, noble knight, I pray forbear,
And do not make remarks on me,
For tomorrow morning I'm to be wed
And my true love shall be in your stead."

6. Twas then he made a solemn vow,
That he would have her whether or no,
This he said to frighten Joan,
As she sat milking all alone:

7. "Oh don't you think these stooks of hay
A pretty place for us to play?
So come with me like a sweet young thing,
And I'll give you a golden ring."

8. "Give me the gold sir, in my hand
And I will be at your command,
For that will be more good to me,
Than twenty husbands," said she.

9. While he looked round for a bed
She mounted on his milk white steed.
He called, he called, 'twas all in vain,
Joan, she never looked back again.

10. She did not think herself quite safe
Until she reached her true love's gate,
She'd robbed him of his steed and gold,
And left him the empty purse to hold.

11. It pleased her lover to the heart,
To think how well she played her part:
"Tomorrow morning we'll be wed,
And I will be the knight instead."

The fragments of words collected from William Hurr are recognisable as a part of a fairly standard set, telling the story of a smart double-dealing girl: a familiar theme in a number of folksongs. Vaughan Williams noted a couple of minor variations to the tune together with a couple of verses in the *Journal of the Folk Song Society* in1913. The text here has been completed from a broadside printed by John Whiting of Birmingham in the nineteenth century. Vaughan Williams published a version of this song that he collected from Christopher Jay in Acle, Norfolk in 1908 in *The Penguin Book of English Folk Songs* (first published in 1959), where the text was completed from a version collected by Cecil Sharp. The melody was also incorporated into his composition *Fantasia on Greensleeves* in 1934. The song was also collected in Sussex and Somerset and is thought to originate in an early ballad entitled *The Baffled Knight*.

For performance in the Blyth Valley Voices project, Chris Coe chose to omit the first verse, and replace verses 5 and 7 above with the following:

"Stop, now stop, noble knight," says she,
"Don't you go making such remarks to me,
Tomorrow morning I'm going to be wed
And my love shall enjoy my maidenhead."

"Then put the ring into my hand,
And I will neither stay nor stand,
For that will be more good to me
Than twenty maidenheads," said she.

In verse 9 she incorporated some words from another version by repeating the last two melody lines:

She robbed him of his horse and ring
And left him raging in the meadows green.

Three Jolly Butchers

1. As Ibsen, Gibson, Johnson, as I've heard many say,
They stole five thousand guineas all on one market day.

2. As they rode over Northumberland as hard as they could ride,
"Oh stop your horse," says Johnson, "I heard a woman cry."

3. So Johnson he got off his horse and viewed the place all round.
He saw a naked woman with her hair pinned to the ground.

4. "How came you here?" cries Johnson, "how came you here?" cries he,
"Two highwaymen have robbed me, as you may plainly see."

5. Now Johnson was a valiant man, a man of courage bold,
He took the coat from off his back, to keep her from the cold.

6. Johnson being a valiant man, a man of valiant mind,
He sat her upon his horse, and he mounted up behind.

7. As they rode along the way as fast as they could ride,
She put her fingers to her lips and gave three piercing cries.

8. And then there came ten swaggering blades with weapons in their hands,
Came riding after Johnson and boldly bade him stand.

9. Now Johnson showed his glittering sword, with all his might and main,
He fought those robbing highwaymen till eight of them were slain.

10. But as he fought the other two, the woman he did not mind,
She took a knife all from his side and stabbed him from behind.

11. But the day it being a market day, and people passing by,
They saw this woman's dreadful deed and raised the hue and cry.

12. "You shall be hanged in chains of gold for the murder you have done,
For you have killed the finest butcher that ever the sun shone on."

This song dates from the seventeenth century, and remained in print throughout the eighteenth and nineteenth centuries: some of the earlier versions locate the actions in Norfolk. Vaughan Williams had previously collected this song from James Punt in Horndon, Essex on one of his earliest collecting trips, in 1904, but still noted down most of the words from William Hurr when he sang it six years later. The words here are mainly Hurr's, supplemented from the version collected from Frank Stockley in Dorset by Henry and Robert Hammond in the 1900s. It is easy to sing the penultimate note as a B flat here, but Vaughan Williams took extra care to note that William Hurr sang it as a B natural. This song has also been collected in Suffolk from Bob Scarce in Blaxhall, and in Norfolk from Ben Baxter in Southrepps, Harry Cox in Catfield and Walter Pardon in Knapton as well as further afield.

When I was Bound Apprentice

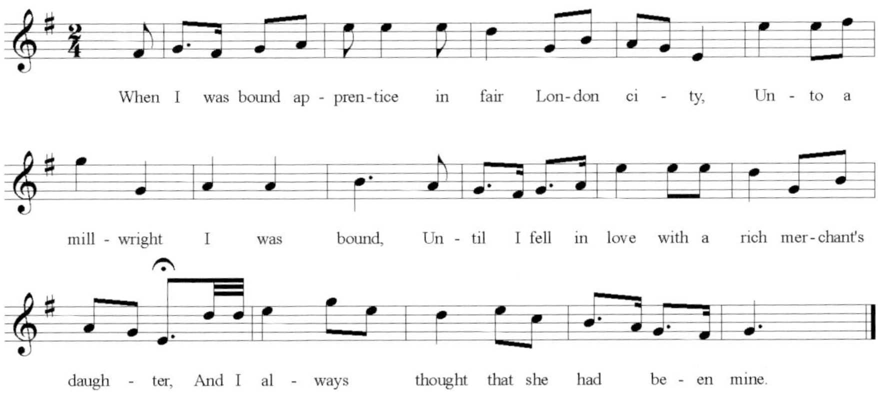

1. When I was bound apprentice in fair London City,
Unto a millwright I was bound,
Until I fell in love with a rich merchant's daughter,
And I always thought that she had been mine.

2. Until that her father he came to know,
He threw me into prison so confined,
Until he kept my true love so long time from me,
And I felt most distracted in my mind.

3. I went up to her parents' house about the hour of eight,
Little did they think that it should be her fate.
I asked her if she'd walk through the fields and meadows gay,
And there we told the tales of love and fixed the wedding day.

4. As we were walking and talking of different things around,
I drew a stick and knocked that fair maid down,
Down on her bended knees she fell, and aloud she for mercy cried,
"Spare the life of an innocent girl, I'm not fit to die."

5. I took her by the curly locks and dragged her to the ground,
Till I came to the river that flowed through Ekefield Town,
It ran both long and narrow, it ran both deep and wide,
And there I plunged this fair maid that should have been my bride.

6. I went home to my parents' house about ten at night,
My mother jumped out of bed all for to light the light,
She asked me, and she questioned me,
"What stains your hands and clothes?"
And the answer I gave: "I've been bleeding through the nose."

7. No rest, no rest all that long night, no rest could I find,
The fire and the brimstone around my head did shine,
It was just two days after, this fair young maid was found,
A-floating by the river that flowed through Ekefield Town.

8. The judges and the jury, on me they did agree,
For this murder, hang-ed I shall be,
O hang-ed, oh hang-ed, oh hang-ed I shall be,
For the murder of this pretty fair maid, hang-ed I shall be.

Vaughan Williams noted down only the first two verses from William Hurr, which were published in the Journal of the Folk Song Society in 1913. With such a wonderful tune, we have tried hard to identify a set of words to complete the song, but it has proved a difficult task.

There are at least two stories told under titles such as *The London Apprentice Boy.* One version, which was sung by Harry Cox from Catfield in Norfolk under the title *Ekefield Town* (the first line of which is very similar to William Hurr's), tells the story of the murder of a young woman, and was first printed in the eighteenth century under the title *The Berkshire Tragedy or The Wittam Miller*. The other, a version of which was sung by Dick Woolnough in Blaxhall, Suffolk, (recorded on the Topic LP *Sing Say and Play* 12TS375) tells the story of an apprentice robbing his master and being transported, a method of punishment in which the guilty party was shipped out to Australia, usually for seven years (in earlier times Virginia was the destination) and which finally came to an end in 1867. It is estimated that during the eighteenth century, over a third of the criminals hanged at Tyburn (see also *In London Town I Was Bred and Born*, page 24) were apprentices, which perhaps accounts for the many songs featuring their wrongdoings.

There is little to link William Hurr's song with either of these songs. The mention of a miller is the strongest link, and together with the fact that his first line is similar, we have chosen Harry Cox's set of words to put to the Southwold tune, but have kept Hurr's first two verses.

Although the song tells of a particularly brutal murder, it has remained popular in oral culture, and perhaps surprisingly, has often been sung by women, including Cecilia Costello from Birmingham, Phoebe Smith, a Traveller who lived for many years outside Woodbridge in Suffolk, and Amy Birch, another Traveller settled in Devon.

Robert Hurr

Robert Watson Hurr (1855-1934), fourth son of William and Maria, married to Elizabeth and father of six children, was also a fisherman, and in later years worked in partnership with his son William Walter Robert (known as Walter). After the Second World War, Walter co-owned the boat *Daisy* with Ben's son: these appear to be the last two of the family to be working fishermen. After the First World War one of Robert's five daughters, Annie, kept a pub, the Royal, in Victoria Street with her husband Arthur Brown. This was just across the road from Robert's house, which was a couple of doors from William's and around the corner from Ben's.

Robert was the only one in the family known to have played an instrument, and as such, would have been in demand at family gatherings and local parties. His repertoire no doubtincluded dance tunes, such as schottisches, polkas or waltzes for couple dances, hornpipes for stepdancing and popular song tunes and maybe some hymns.

Robert Hurr (right)
Note the leather thigh boots worn by both fishermen (the man on the left is named Cannell). John Harrington supplied these from his shop in Southwold High Street. Victoria Palmer remembered saying to her new husband Victor, in about 1920: 'Them long leather legs'll kill you, bor,' and explained, 'He was crazed to hev the seaboots made, with the wooden sole right thick and studded … he'd keep 'em in the water butt through the good days, keep 'em sorft … but I told him, lad, I said, them long leather legs'll kill you, bor.' They didn't, but others were indeed drowned, hampered by the weight of water in the long boots when unlucky enough to go into the water.

Photograph by Frederick Jenkins, courtesy of Andrew Jenkins

Robert Hurr (right, aged 77) and his son Walter aboard their boat the *Boy Billy* in 1932. The boat is moored in the river, and shrimp nets and oars can be seen on board. *Boy Billy* was nearly 50 years old, and had an engine fitted only a couple of years before this picture was taken.

Photograph courtesy of Gary May

The Royal George

1. As we set sail for the Rock of Gibraltar,
As we set sail from sweet Dublin Bay,
Oh little did we think of our sad misfortune,
A-sleeping in the briny sea.
Refrain:
Oh little did we think of our sad misfortune,
A-sleeping in the briny sea.

2. Oh there was one poor woman a-living in the city;
As soon as she heard that her husband was dead,
It filled her poor heart with grief and pain,
So hear what that poor woman said.
Refrain:
It filled her poor heart with grief and pain,
So hear what that poor woman said.

3. She said: "I'll go and seek for my own true lover,
I'll go and sail the wide world round;
Then if my own true lover I do not discover,
All in some salt seas I will drown."
Refrain:
"Then if my own true lover I do not discover,
All in some salt seas I will drown."

Roy Palmer in *Folk Songs Collected by Ralph Vaughan Williams* speculates that this song may relate to the Battle of Sole Bay in 1672; although the Earl of Sandwich's ship was the Royal James, not the Royal George, this could have been a case of mishearing the title. The Royal George itself had a rather ignominious end, which proved tragic for the hundreds of crew and visitors aboard, when in 1782, during the course of some repair work, she sank in the English Channel near Portsmouth, with the loss of all fourteen hundred people on board.

Bold Princess Royal

1. On the fourteenth of February we sailed from the land
In the bold Princess Royal bound for Newfoundland,
We had forty bright seamen for a ship's company,
And boldly from the eastward to westward bore we.

2. We had not been sailing past days two or three;
When a man from our masthead a sail he did see,
She came bearing down on us to see what we were,
While under her mizzen black colours she wore.

3. "Good Lord," cried the captain, "what shall we do now?
Here comes the bold pirate, to rob us I know."
"Oh no," cried our chief mate, "that shall never be so,
We'll shake out a reef boys, and from her we will go."

4. Now when this bold pirate she hove alongside,
With a long speaking trumpet, "Whence come you?" he cried,
Our captain being aft boys, he answered them so,
"We came from fair London, we're bound for Cairo."

5. "Come haul up your courses and heave your ship to,
For I have a letter I'll send home by you."
"I will haul up my courses, and heave my ship to,
But it shall be in some harbour and not alongside you."

6. "Come hoist up your topsails, your staysails too,
Top gallant sails and royals, boys, and from her we will go."
They fired shots after us but could not prevail,
When the bold Princess Royal soon showed them her tail.

7. She chased us to windward for all that long day,
She chased us to windward, but she could make no way,
She chased us to windward, when she could make no way
So she hauled up her mainsail and then bore away.

8. Thank God cried our captain, since the pirate is gone,
Go down to your grog, boys, go down every one,
Go down to your grog, boys, and be of good cheer,
For while we have sea-room, my boys, never harm.

Two tunes were noted for this song by Vaughan Williams on his first day in Southwold, but no words. A closer look at Butterworth's manuscripts reveal that this unusual variant of the tune was sung by Robert Hurr, whilst William sang the more standard version of the tune, also commonly used for the song *Flash Company* in East Anglia. The song is widespread and particularly popular in seagoing communities on the east coast: versions have been collected in Suffolk from Harold Smy, Jumbo Brightwell and Bob Roberts, and in Norfolk from Sam Larner and Walter Pardon and was one of the songs Vaughan Williams had noted down from Charles Pottipher in Ingrave, Essex in December 1903 during his earliest experiences of listening to traditional singers. The texts of all oral versions are very similar; the words given here are based on a broadside printed by Hodges in London in the nineteenth century. It is interesting to note that although Vaughan Williams and Butterworth both heard Robert Hurr sing this on 24th October 1910. Butterworth gave the song a rather more jaunty feel in his interpretation that day, as can be seen below.

In London Town I Was Bred and Born

1. In London town I was bred and born;
In Tyburn's ground there I died of scorn.
I served my time to a saddler's trade,
I was always counted but a roving blade.

2. For at seventeen I took a wife:
I loved her dearly as I loved my life.
For to maintain her both fine and gay
I took up a robbing on the king's highway.

3. I robbed Lords and Dukes, I do declare,
And lovely Nancy with the golden hair.
We shuttered the shutters, bid them goodnight,
And carried the gold to our heart's delight.

4. Through Covent Garden I took my way
With my pretty blowen to see the play,
Till Fielding's gang did me pursue:
Taken I was by that cursed crew.

5. But when I'm dead and carried to my grave,
A pleasant funeral let me have;
Six highwaymen to carry me -
Give them broadswords and sweet liberty.

6. Six blooming girls to bear my pall -
Give them white gloves and pink ribbons all.
When I'm dead they may tell the truth:
There goes a wild and a wicked youth.

The first verse is the only one noted down by Vaughan Williams from Robert Hurr. The song is also known under a variety of other titles including *Wild and Wicked Youth, The Flash Lad* and *Adieu Adieu*, and sung in Ireland where London is frequently replaced by Newry. In East Anglia it has been recorded from Bob Scarce in Suffolk and Sam Larner, Walter Pardon, Harry Cox and Elijah Bell in Norfolk. It was also collected widely in the USA.

Tyburn, situated near Marble Arch in London, was the scene of thousands of hangings for five hundred or so years until the late eighteenth century, and was a popular place for an outing! As a result, many ballads were written and sold by hawkers both at the event and afterwards, purporting to be the last words of the dying person.

Glossary

Fielding's Gang — This refers to the Bow Street Runners, the first police force to be established in London in 1751, founded by the novelist Henry Fielding and his brother John, both London magistrates at the time.

Blowen — Sweetheart, lover (earlier: harlot)

On Monday Morning I Married a Wife

1. On Monday morning I married a wife,
Thinking to lead a sober life, *(repeat first two lines)*
I wished in my heart I had been dead,
Before I enjoyed her maidenhead.
Chorus: Sing fol de lol lay, Sing fol de lol day.

2. So on Tuesday morning I went to the wood,
Thinking to do my wife some good;
I cut off a twig of holly so green,
As fine a twig as ever was seen.
Chorus

3. So on Wednesday morning I hung it to dry,
And on Thursday morning I did it try:
I laid on her back and I laid on her wig,
Until I'd broken my holly twig.
Chorus

4. On Friday morning to my surprise,
A little before the sun did rise,
She opened her mouth and begun to roar,
And I thought in my heart she'd never give o'er.
Chorus

5. On Saturday morning she began her game;
I beat her till she was blind and lame,
The devil came in at the height of the game,
And stole her away both blind and lame.
Chorus

6. So on Sunday noon I dined in state,
Without a scolding wife or howling mate;
Now I'm enjoying my bottle and friend,
And what do you think of my jolly week's end?
Chorus

This song has proved very difficult to identify, as Vaughan Williams noted down no words to this song, and also seemed uncertain about the title, which he noted as *The Tiresome Wife* (but with a question mark), whilst George Butterworth noted it down as *On Monday Morning I Married a Wife*. A broadside text exists entitled *The Gossiping Wife,* but neither this nor other collected versions of *On Monday Morning I Married Wife* fit the tune collected in Southwold! The text above is quite heavily adapted from the version noted by Vaughan Williams from a Mr. Hilton in South Walsham in Norfolk on a visit in April 1908, and is one possible solution to the conundrum. It was published under the title *The Holly Twig* in *Folk Songs Collected by Ralph Vaughan Williams*. Readers and singers keen to delve further are referred to the sources listed in the section of this book titled Further Information on page 44.

Although the tone of the lyrics may not be to contemporary tastes, the song seems to have been popular in the early years of the twentieth century as Vaughan Williams and many of his folk song collecting colleagues, including the prolific folk song collector Cecil Sharp, Percy Grainger, Sabine Baring-Gould and George Gardiner, collected a number of versions around the country. The song has several alternative titles including *A Week's Work Well Done*, *The Holly Twig* and *When I Was A Batchelor* and was also popular in north America.

Robert Hurr's Hornpipe

Vaughan Williams did not often write down instrumental pieces, and this is the only one he noted whilst in Southwold. In his manuscript it is titled *The Liverpool Hornpipe.* Whether this was his name for it or Robert Hurr's is not known, but the tune is nothing like the usual tune of that name and is actually a variant of what is perhaps the most widely-known hornpipe of all, *Soldier's Joy.* Robert played the concertina according to Vaughan Williams' notes, but it is not known whether it was an Anglo, English or Duet system. Vaughan Williams noted the tune in the key of F, whilst Butterworth sets it in B flat: the notes are the same, but the structure and accompanying chords suggest B flat as the more natural key signature. We have given Butterworth's notaion here and also provided a version transposed into D, which is the standard key for *Soldier's Joy* across the United Kingdom and north America.

Hornpipes were, and still are, commonly used for 'stepping': an informal, improvised form of tap dancing, usually danced solo and particularly popular amongst fishermen on the east coast. It is therefore extremely likely that Robert would have played for such dancing in the pubs and taprooms of Southwold.

Ben Hurr

Benjamin Lowsey Hurr (1860 -1934), the seventh of William and Maria's eleven children who lived to adulthood, married Louisa and had one son. In the 1890s, along with brothers William and Robert, he was a member of the lifeboat crew. In the early twentieth century Ben and his family moved out of the small fishermen's cottages in Victoria Street into one of the newer terraces in the north end of the town.

Lifeboat Day, 1908
Photograph by Frederick Jenkins, courtesy of Southwold Museum

The Isle of France

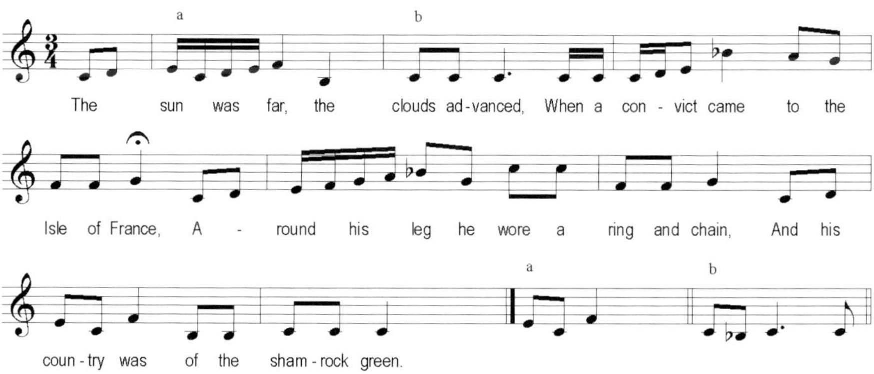

1. The sun was far, the clouds advanced,
When a convict came to the Isle of France;
Around his leg he wore a ring and chain,
And his country was of the shamrock green.

2. The coastguard waited all on the beach,
Till the convict's boat was all in reach;
The convict's chains did so shine and spark,
Which touched the coast-guard to the very heart.

3. Then the coastguard launched his little boat,
That on the ocean with him did float
The birds at night take their silent rest,
But the convict here has a wounded breast.

4. When the coastguard came to the Isle of France,
Towards him the convict did advance,
Then the tears from his eyes did fall like rain,
"Young man, I hear you are of the shamrock green."

5. "I am a shamrock," the convict cried,
"That has been toss'd on the ocean wide,
For being unruly I do declare,
And was doomed to transport for seven years.

6. "When six of them was past and gone,
We were coming home to make up for one,
When the stormy winds did blow and roar,
Which cast me here on a foreign shore."

7. Then the coastguard played a noble part,
And with some brandy cheered the convict's heart;
"Although the night is so advanced,
You shall find a friend in the Isle of France."

8. Then a speedy letter went to the Queen,
About the dreadful shipwreck of the Shamrock green;
Then his freedom came by a speedy post,
To the absent convict they thought was lost.

9. "God bless the coastguard," the convict cried,
"You have saved my life from the ocean wide;
I will drink to his health in a flowing glass,
And here's success to the Isle of France."

Vaughan Williams noted down no words to this song, also known as *The Convict Shamrock Green*, perhaps aware that there were several sets of words printed on broadsides: the text here is that printed by Disley of St Giles, London, with one or two small amendments for clarity in performance. A version collected from Frederick Rolfe is published in Lilias Rider Haggard's book *I Walked by Night*: the poacher made famous by this publication of his memoirs was also a singer of old songs and lived just outside Bungay in the early 1900s. Rolfe's words are very similar, but start from the point of view of the man's sweetheart left behind when he is transported. The 'Isle of France' is an old name for Mauritius, an island in the Indian Ocean colonized by the French between 1721 and 1810.

Jones's Ale

1. The first to come in was a dyer,
He sat himself down by the fire,
He sat himself down by the fire,
Amongst the jovial crew,
He told the landlord to his face
That the chimney corner should be his place,
And there he would sit and dye his own face,
When Jones's ale was new.

Chorus:
When Jones's ale was new, brave boys,
When Jones's ale was new.

2. The next to come in was a bricklayer,
And he was a jolly bricklayer,
And he was a jolly bricklayer,
Amongst the jovial crew,
He pitched his trowel against the wall,
He wished the steeples and towers might fall,
It would make work for bricklayers all,
When Jones's ale was new.

3. The next to come in was a cobbler,
And he was a jolly cobbler,
And he was a jolly cobbler,
Amongst the jovial crew,
Fetch out your boots, he'll mend your shoes,
He'll mend your slippers as good as new -
Look how his awl goes through and through,
When Jones's ale was new.

4. The next to come in was a tinker,
And he was no small beer drinker,
And he was no small beer drinker,
Amongst the jovial crew,
Fetch out your pots and tins and kettles -
His rivets are made of the very best metal,
Hark how his old hammer does bang and rattle.
When Jones's ale was new.

5. The next to come in was a blacksmith,
And he was a jolly blacksmith,
And he was a jolly blacksmith,
Amongst the jovial crew,
He swore he'd make a hook and hoe,
His queer old hammer went high and low,
And how his old bellows did puff and blow.
When Jones's ale was new.

6. The next to come in was a soldier,
With his firelock over his shoulder,
With his firelock over his shoulder,
Amongst the jovial crew.
He swore he'd fight for old England's crown,
Before the old country should be put down,
And every man gave him half-a-crown.
When Jones's ale was new.

Vaughan Williams noted down six verses of this song and made the comment that the chorus was sung 'only occasionally'. He had also collected this song a couple of years earlier from a Mr. Hilton in South Walsham, Norfolk in 1908. (see also *On Monday Morning I married a Wife* on page 25 /26) .*Jones's Ale* (or sometimes *Joan's Ale)* is one of the most ancient songs still to be in currency amongst singers, dating back to at least 1594 and remaining in print throughout the subsequent centuries. It has been recorded in East Anglia from Charlie Stringer in Suffolk (VT C2CD) Walter Pardon in Norfolk and Harry Green in Essex, as well as from the Copper Family in Sussex and Fred Jordan in Shropshire.

George Butterworth's manuscripts contain a version noted from Robert Hurr, with a very similar tune. He noted five verses from Robert including the three below which are quite different to those sung by younger brother Ben. The first one makes a nice introduction to all the verses about the various tradesmen.

It's of three jolly tradesmen,
They all fell out a-drinking,
They all fell out a-drinking,
Among the joyful crew,
As he sat down to be merry,
He called for a bottle of sherry.
And then they sat and drank so merry.

Chorus:
When Jones's ale was new, brave boys,
When Jones's ale was new.

The next to come in was a hatter,
He wants to know what's the matter,
He wants to know what's the matter,
Among the joyful crew,
He waved his hat all on the ground,
That every man should spend a crown,
He sat and drank their health all round.
Chorus

The next to come in was a tailor,
He swore he'd be no sailor,
He swore he'd be no sailor,
Among the joyful crew,
He sat and he called for all and joked,
Till this poor tailor he was broke,
And he was obliged to pawn his coat,
Chorus

The Cobbler

1. A story, a story to you I will tell,
Concerning of a butcher who in London Town did dwell,
Now the butcher he possessed a charming little wife,
And she loved the little cobbler, she loved him as her life,
Chorus: To my fal-da-riddle-i-doh, tiddy-fa-lal-the-day.

2. Now the butcher went to market to purchase an ox,
The cunning little cobbler as sly as any fox,
Put on his Sunday clothing a courting for to go,
To the jolly butcher's wife, because he loved her so, *Chorus*

3. The cobbler walking down the street stepped in the butcher's shop,
The butcher's wife knew what he meant and bid him for to stop,
He said, "My little darling have you a job for me?"
The butcher's wife so smiling said, "I'll go upstairs and see".*Chorus*

4. She went up to the bedroom and gave the snob a call,
Saying, "I have found a job for you, if you have brought your awl,
And if you do it workman-like some cash to you I'll pay,"
"I thank you," said the cobbler and began to stitch away. *Chorus*

5. Now while the cobbler was at work a knock came at the door,
The cobbler crawled beneath the bed and laid upon the floor,
"Lay still," said the butcher's wife, "What will my husband say?"
Then she let the policeman in along with her to play. *Chorus*

6.The butcher came from market and put them in a fright,
The policeman quickly ran down stairs and soon was out of sight,
The butcher's wife so nimbly locked up the bedroom door
And in her plight she quite forgot the cobbler on the floor. *Chorus*

7.And that night the butcher was lying in the bed,
"There's something here is very hard," the butcher smiled and said,
She said, "It is my rolling pin," the butcher gave a laugh,
Saying, "How come you roll your dough with a policeman's staff? *Chorus*

8.The butcher flung the truncheon underneath the bed,
There it broke the chamber-pot and cracked the cobbler's head;
The cobbler shouted "Murder," the butcher said, "Who are you?"
"I am the little cobbler that comes to mend the lady's shoe." *Chorus*

9."If you're the little cobbler, you come along with me,
I'll pay you well for mending shoes before I've done with thee,"
He locked him in his bull's pen, the bull began to roar,
The butcher laughed to see him toss the cobbler o'er and o'er. *Chorus*

10.Early next morning when people were about,
The butcher rubbed his face in blood and let the cobbler out,
He pinned a ticket on his back and on it was the news,
"I am the little cobbler come to mend the ladies shoes. *Chorus*

11.The cobbler was so frightened, home he quickly ran,
His coat and breeches were so torn, he nearly showed his bum;
His anxious wife did meet him and he shouted out, " Oh Lor'!
My dear," he said, "I'll never go out stitching any more". *Chorus*

Vaughan Williams noted no words from Ben Hurr, perhaps as he had heard the song before, in 1904 when Mr James Punt of East Horndon, near Brentwood in Essex had sung it to him. The song has also been collected elsewhere in Suffolk, from Tom Smith of Thorpe Morieux near Lavenham and Tom's words, which he got from his father, are used here. Elsewhere in East Anglia it has been recorded from Alec Bloomfield (near Saxmundham in Suffolk) and Walter Pardon from Norfolk. Vaughan Williams described the song when publishing it in the English Folk Dance and Song Society's Journal in 1906 as: " a modern example of the kind of rough fun which we find in Chaucer's *Clerk of Oxenforde*", presumably taking the presence of the policeman as evidence of its relative modernity.

Glossary:

Snob cobbler

The Rich Old Farmer

1. It's of a rich old farmer who lived in Derbyshire,
He had one only daughter, most beautiful and fair,
He had one only daughter, rich, handsome, kind and free,
And it's many a wealthy farmer's son would have gained her company.

2. It's of a rich young squire who lived there close by,
He swore he would not be easy until he had a try,
So he dressed himself as a tinker and travelled all on his way,
Till at last he came to the old farmhouse, and these are the words he did say:

3. "Bring out your pots and kettles, and any old tins to mend;
Or have you any lodgings for me, a single young man?"
"Oh, yes," replied this pretty maid, not thinking any harm,
"You're welcome to stay here all night if you sleep in my father's barn."

4. Then supper being over she went out to make his bed -
He quickly followed after and stole her maidenhead,
She, being brisk and lively, jumped up and barred the door,
And she slept all night in her tinker's arms among the barley straw.

5. "Now since you've had your will of me, pray tell to me your name,
Where's your occupation and where and whence you came?"
He softly whispered in her ear. "Pray call me David Shaw,
And if ever I come this way again, remember the barley straw."

Vaughan Williams noted down a full set of words for this song, although unfortunately omitted to write down which of the Hurr brothers sang it to him! Many versions of the song end with the girl falling pregnant, and 'shame' and 'gossip' are mentioned in the text, but the Southwold singer seemed content to describe a somewhat happier situation where the girl does not seem to suffer at all. Roy Palmer in *Folk Songs collected by Ralph Vaughan Williams* relates it to a ballad in Samuel Pepys' collection of broadsides, *The Pollitick Beggar-Man* and it certainly dates from at least the eighteenth century. It has been collected in the west country and was clearly popular in Norfolk, where it was noted from Ben Baxter in Southrepps, Harry Cox in Catfield and Bill Lowne in Cley-next-the-Sea.

Charles Newby

On Tuesday 25th October Vaughan Williams and Butterworth cycled over to Reydon, to the Almshouses and noted two songs from a Mr. Newby. Charles Newby, then aged 79, was born in Sotherton but lived most of his life in Southwold . He kept the White Horse Inn at the Reydon end of the High Street for many years and was later a coal merchant when he lived at 13, Station Road, in the left hand house of a pair known as Gladstone Villas.

Georgey

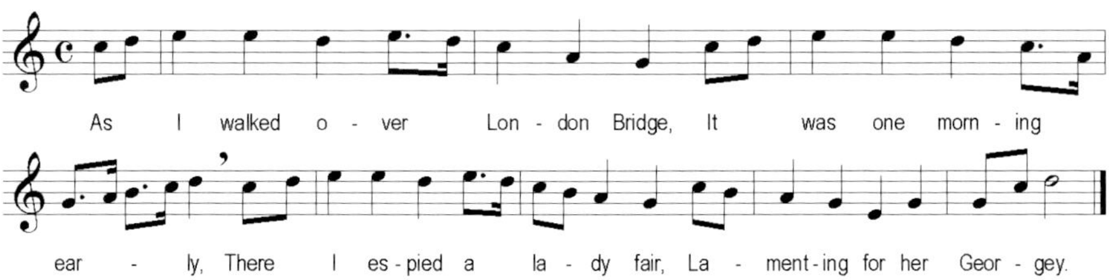

1. As I walked over London Bridge,
It was one morning early,
There I espied a lady fair,
Lamenting for her Georgey.

2. "Come fetch to me some little boy,
That can run an errand gaily,
That can run for ten miles in one hour,
With a letter for a lady.

3. "Come saddle me my milk white steed,
Come saddle it so neatly,
That I may go down to Newcastle Gaol,
Begging for the life of my Georgey."

4. But when she came to Newcastle gaol,
She bowed her head so slowly,
Three times on her bended knees did fall,
Saying, "Spare me the life of Georgey."

5. The judge looked over his left shoulder,
And he seemed very hard hearted;
He said, "My dear you must be gone,
For there is no pardon granted."

6. "It is no murder Georgey has done,
Nor has he killed any,
But stolen sixteen of the King's best steeds
And sold them in Bohemia.

7. Six pretty babies I have born
And the seventh lies in my body,
I'd freely part with them every one,
If you'd spare me the life of Georgey."

8. The judge looked over his left shoulder
And he seemed very sorry,
He said, "My dear you are too late,
Georgey's condemned already."

9. "My George shall be hung in chains of gold,
Of such there are not many,
Because he was come of noble breed,
And was loved by a virtuous lady.

10. I wish I was on yonder hill,
Where times I have been many,
With sword and pistol by my side,
I'd fight for the life of Georgey."

Vaughan Williams collected this song on several occasions, including versions from Fowlmere and Fen Ditton in Cambridgeshire on earlier collecting trips in 1906 and 1907. On the occasion when Charles Newby sang it, George Butterworth noted down the tune, which was subsequently published in the English Folk Dance and Song Society's Journal in 1913. The words here are supplied from a broadside printed in Herefordshire between 1825-42, as no words were noted down by either Butterworth or Vaughan Williams. The song is well-known across both England and Scotland, and has a number of ancient antecedents: a ballad about the true story of George Gordon, Earl of Huntley in 1554, and broadside versions from the seventeenth century variously relating the stories of George Stoole from Northumberland and 'George of Oxenforde'.

Forty Miles

1. On yonder hill and there it stood,
A neat little cottage near to the wood,
Where I have never been,
Oh, where I have never been.

2. And it's at hand and far from town,
The rain fell first and the sun was gone down,
So I begged to be let in. *(repeat)*

3. "Oh no, kind sir, that never can be,
There's no one in this house but me,
And I'd rather you be gone." *(repeat)*

4. That rains, that hails, that whistles on high,
The clouds are black, no stars in the sky,
So I begged, "Love let me in." *(repeat)*

5. Then kind compassion serves her so,
She could not bear to see him go,
So she called him back again. *(repeat)*

6. So when that him she had let in,
He told her that her heart he'd win,
And he'd make her his lawful bride. *(repeat)*

7. So the very next morning to church they went,
And married they were, with sweet content,
And he made her his lawful bride. *(repeat)*

This song is also known as *The Cottage By the Wood* and is related to another called *Cold, Haily Rainy Night.* It has also been collected in Yorkshire and Somerset, but not in the eastern counties, the nearest other source being Harry Scott, recorded by Fred Hamer in Bedfordshire.

Vaughan Williams noted down all the words above, and indicated that verse three could be repeated between verses four and five. For performance in the Blyth Valley Voices project, Chris Coe added the linking 'Oh' for the repeated line, and also two extra verses collected in Somerset by Robert and Henry Hammond from a Mrs. Gulliver in 1905. These may be added after verse five and seven respectively:

You take off your wet and put on your dry,
You go into bed and quietly lie,
And quickly I'll be there. *(repeat)*

Come all young men whoever you be,
Kiss all the pretty girls that ever you see,
They'll call you back again. *(repeat)*

Almshouses, Reydon
These almshouses with their charmingly rustic appearance were built in 1908 by the benefactor Andrew Matthews of Southwold. Charles Newby was one of the first tenants.

Martha Cable

On the first of their two day visit, Vaughan Williams and Butterworth went to the small village of Shadingfield, on the main road to Beccles. There Butterworth noted down the tune to one song from a 'Mrs Keble aged 84', and Vaughan Williams wrote down the words to a toast by Mr Keble. Records for Shadingfield in the early twentieth century show no-one by the name of Keble, although it is a common Suffolk name, but there was a Martha Cable living there in 1901, aged 70, widow of farm worker George Cable, and living with her was her unmarried son Frederick, then aged 33. It seems more than likely that these are the people Vaughan Williams and Butterworth visited in 1910. It was evidently a somewhat disappointing trip, as the only song noted down from Mrs Cable was *The Murder of Maria Marten,* which Vaughan Williams had collected before, and which he left to Butterworth to note down on this occasion.

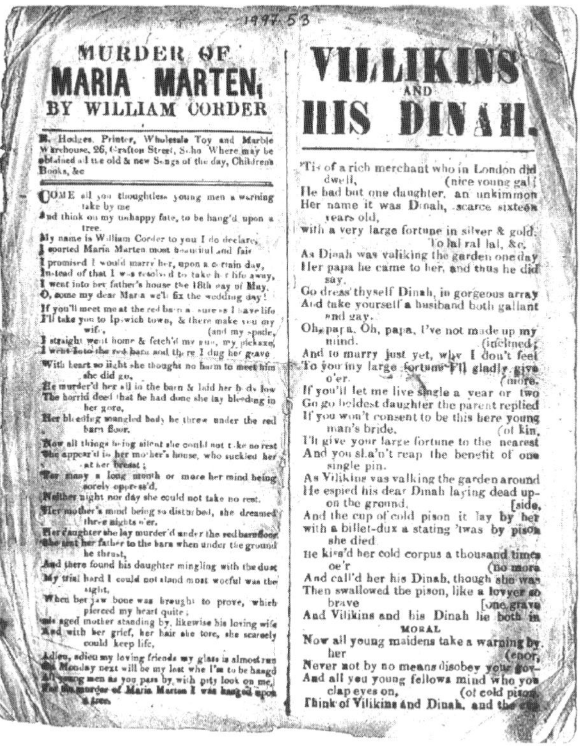
1997.53

MURDER OF
MARIA MARTEN,
BY WILLIAM CORDER

H. Hodges, Printer, Wholesale Toy and Marble Warehouse, 26, Grafton Street, Soho Where may be obtained all the old & new Songs of the day, Children's Books, &c

COME all you thoughtless young men a warning take by me
And think on my unhappy fate, to be hang'd upon a tree.
My name is William Corder to you I do declare,
I courted Maria Marten most beautiful and fair
I promised I would marry her, upon a certain day,
Instead of that I was resolved to take her life away,
I went into her father's house the 18th day of May,
O, come my dear Maria we'll fix the wedding day!
If you'll meet me at the red barn as sure as I have life
I'll take you to Ipswich town, & there make you my wife, (and my spade,
I straight went home & fetch'd my gun, my pickaxe,
I went into the red barn and there I dug her grave
With heart so light she thought no harm to meet him she did go,
He murder'd her all in the barn & laid her body low
The horrid deed that he had done she lay bleeding in her gore,
Her bleeding mangled body he threw under the red barn floor.
Now all things being silent she could not take no rest
She appear'd in her mother's house, who suckled her at her breast;
For many a long month or more her mind being sorely oppress'd,
Neither night nor day she could not take no rest.
Her mother's mind being so disturbed, she dreamed three nights o'er,
Her daughter she lay murder'd under the red barn floor,
She sent her father to the barn when under the ground he thrust,
And there found his daughter mingling with the dust
My trial hard I could not stand most woeful was the sight,
When her jaw bone was brought to prove, which pierced my heart quite;
His aged mother standing by, likewise his loving wife
And with her grief, her hair she tore, she scarcely could keep life,
Adieu, adieu my loving friends my glass is almost run
On Monday next will be my last whe I'm to be hangd
All young men as you pass by, with pity look on me,
For the murder of Maria Marten I was hanged upon a tree.

VILLIKINS
AND
HIS DINAH.

'Tis of a rich merchant who in London did dwell, (nice young gal;
He had but one daughter, an unkimmon
Her name it was Dinah, scarce sixteen years old,
with a very large fortune in silver & gold.
To lal ral lal, &c.
As Dinah was valiking the garden one day
Her papa he came to her, and thus he did say.
Go dress thyself Dinah, in gorgeous array
And take yourself a husiband both gallant and gay.
Oh, papa, Oh, papa, I've not made up my mind. (inclined;
And to marry just yet, why I don't feel
To your my large fortune I'll gladly give o'er. (more.
If you'll let me live single a year or two
Go go boldest daughter the parent replied
If you won't consent to be this here young man's bride. (of kin,
I'll give your large fortune to the nearest
And you shan't reap the benefit of one single pin.
As Vilikins vas valking the garden around
He espied his dear Dinah laying dead upon the ground. [side,
And the cup of cold pison it lay by her
with a billet-dux a stating 'twas by pison she died
He kiss'd her cold corpus a thousand times oe'r (no more
And call'd her his Dinah, though she was
Then swallowed the pison, like a lovyer so brave [one grave
And Vilikins and his Dinah lie both in
MORAL
Now all young maidens take a warning by her (enor,
Never not by no means disobey your gov-
And all you young fellows mind who you clap eyes on, (of cold pison.
Think of Vilikins and Dinah, and the cup

Broadsheet containing *The Murder of Maria Marten.* This was produced by the broadside printer Hodges of London, and purports to contain the murderer, William Corder's last words in the shape of a song. Another version, printed by J. Catnach, also contains Corder's confession in narrative form. No tune is indicated, but it is usually song to the tune of Dives and Lazarus, and it may be that other printed versions suggested this tune, as its use is very widespread for this song.

Courtesy of St Edmundsbury Borough Council – Moyse's Hall Museum

Maria Martin

1. Come all you thoughtless young men, a warning take by me,
And think on my unhappy fate to be hanged upon a tree:
My name is William Corder, to you I do declare,
I courted Maria Marten, most beautiful and fair.

2. I promised I would marry her upon a certain day,
Instead of that, I was resolved to take her life away.
I went into her father's house the eighteenth day of May,
Saying, "My dear Maria, we will fix the wedding day.

3. If you will meet me at the Red Barn, as sure as I have life,
I will take you to Ipswich town, and there make you my wife."
I then went home and fetched my gun, my pickaxe and my spade,
I went into the Red Barn, and there I dug her grave.

4. With heart so light, she thought no harm, to meet him she did go
He murdered her all in the barn, and laid her body low:
After the horrible deed was done, she lay weltering in her gore,
Her bleeding mangled body he buried beneath the Red Barn floor.

5. Now all things being silent, her spirit could not rest,
She appeared unto her mother, who suckled her at her breast;
For many a long month or more, her mind being sore oppressed,
Neither night or day she could not take any rest.

6. Her mother's mind being so disturbed, she dreamt three nights o'er,
Her daughter she lay murdered beneath the Red Barn floor;
She sent the father to the barn, when he the ground did thrust,
And there he found his daughter mingling with the dust.

7. My trial is hard, I could not stand, most woeful was the sight,
When her jaw bone was brought to prove, which pierced my heart quite;
Her aged father standing by, likewise his loving wife,
And in her grief her hair she tore, she scarcely could keep life.

8. Adieu, Adieu, my loving friends, my glass is almost run,
On Monday next will be my last, when I am to be hanged;
So you, young men, who do pass by, with pity look on me,
For murdering Maria Marten, I was hanged upon this tree.

It was George Butterworth who noted down the tune to this song from Mrs Cable. Vaughan Williams had already come across it in Norfolk in 1905, sung by Mr. Whitby of Tilney All Saints, near King's Lynn. In later years Vaughan Williams revisited the tune and wrote 'Five Versions of Dives and Lazarus' (the name of an old ballad using the same tune) when commissioned to write a piece for England for the World's Fair in the USA in 1939. No words were taken down, and the text above is from a broadside printed in the nineteenth century. Freda Palmer, from Witney in Oxfordshire sang the song to the same tune, which is also well-known in Ireland as *The Star of the County Down.*

It is reputed that over a million copies of the broadsheet were sold in the nineteenth century, and the story and ambiguous nature of the evidence inspired a stage melodrama which is still presented in repertory occasionally, followed by a film in 1935 starring Todd Slaughter and in the late twentieth century a television drama. William Corder was indeed hanged for the murder (often referred to as the Red Barn Murder) which took place at Polstead, near Sudbury in Suffolk, and there are some gruesome artefacts to be seen relating to the case in the Moyse's Hall Museum in Bury St Edmunds.

Toast

Health and wealth and golden store,
I wish you in Heaven when you die
What can I wish you more?

This was noted by Vaughan Williams from a 'Mr. Keble' in Shadingfield, who must have been Martha Cable's son, Frederick, then in his early forties. Singing sessions in Suffolk still sometimes feature a toast or two, as a way of bringing together the assembled company. This one seems a fitting item with which to close this collection of songs.

Bibliography

Southwold

Southwold: Portrait of an English Seaside Town, editors R. & S. Clegg, 1999
A Selection of Ghost Stories, Smuggling Stories and Poems connected with Southwold, A.B. Jenkins, 1986
A Photographic Collection of Bygones & Local Characters of Southwold, A.B.Jenkins
A Visit to Southwold, A.B. Jenkins, 1983
The Story of Southwold, Janet Becker, 1948
Southwold in Old Photographs, John Miller, 1999

Folk Song, Vaughan Williams & George Butterworth

Folk Songs Collected by Ralph Vaughan Williams, Roy Palmer, 1983
Whom the Gods Love: George Butterworth, Michael Barlow, 1997
Ralph Vaughan Williams: A Pictorial Biography, Ursula Vaughan Williams, 1971
English Folk-Songs, Ralph Vaughan Williams, 1912
The Ingrave Secret, Frank Dineen, 2001
The Penguin Book of English Folk Songs, editors Ralph Vaughan Williams and A.L. Lloyd, 1959 (due to be reprinted).
Traditional Tunes, Frank Kidson, 1891, reprinted 1999
Journal of the Folk Song Society, Vol iv, number 17, 1913 , English Folk Dance & Song Society
English Dance & Song
Vol 35, No 3 (1972), Vol 39, No 1 (1977) and Vol 45, No 1 (1983), English Folk Dance & Song Society

Further Information on the Songs

For further information on the specific songs contained in this collection, for comparative texts and scores and commentaries, readers are referred to the following sources. Each one provides its own numbering system, and references are given below.

The English and Scottish Popular Ballads, by Frances J. Child
(1882-1898, 5 volumes)

Folk Song Index and *Broadside Index,* by Steve Roud, a regularly updated database available on subscription or at the Vaughan Williams Memorial Library at the English Dance & Song Society (London), the Irish Traditional Music Archive (Dublin) and the School of Scottish Studies (Edinburgh)

American Balladry from British Broadsides, by G. Malcolm Laws (1957)

The Vaughan Williams Memorial Library can be contacted at the English Folk Dance and Song Society, 2 Regent's Park Road, London NW1 7AY.
Telephone 020 7485 2206.

Song References

The Loss of the London Roud 1787

Lovely Joan Roud 592 / Child 112

Three Jolly Butchers Roud 17 / Laws L4

When I Was Bound Apprentice Roud 2630

The Royal George Roud 2529

Bold Princess Royal Roud 528 / Laws K29

In London Town I Was Bred and Born Roud 490 / Laws L12

On Monday Morning I Married a Wife Roud 433 / Laws Q6

The Isle of France Roud 1575

When Jones' Ale Was New Roud 139

The Cobbler Roud 174

The Rich Old Farmer Roud 118 / Child 279

Georgey Roud 90 / Child 209

Forty Miles Roud 608

The Murder of Maria Marten Roud 215

Index